MCO P4790.1

MARINE CORPS
INTEGRATED MAINTENANCE
MANAGEMENT SYSTEM (MIMMS)
INTRODUCTION MANUAL

[MIMMS Introduction Manual]

U. S. MARINE CORPS

PCN 102 065450 00

MCO P4790.1B
LPP-3-dt
17 Mar 1989

MARINE CORPS ORDER P4790.1B W/CH 1 & 2

From: Commandant of the Marine Corps
TO: Distribution List

Subj: Marine Corps Integrated Maintenance Management System
      (MIMMS) Introduction Manual (Short Title: MIMMS
      Introduction Manual)

Encl: (1) LOCATOR SHEET

1. <u>Purpose</u>. To establish the policy for MIMMS and to explain
ground equipment maintenance management in the Marine Corps.

2. <u>Cancellation</u>. MCO P4790.1A.

3. <u>Summary of Revision</u>. This revision contains a substantial
number of changes and should be completely reviewed.

4. <u>Recommendations</u>. Recommendations concerning the contents
of the MIMMS Introduction Manual are invited. Submit recommendations via the appropriate chain of command to the
Commandant of the Marine Corps (CMC) (LPP) for evaluation.

5. <u>Reserve Applicability</u>. This Manual is applicable to the
Marine Corps Reserve.

6. <u>Certification</u>. Reviewed and approved this date.

W. G. CARSON, JR.
Deputy Chief of Staff
for Installations and Logistics

DISTRIBUTION: E14

  Copy to: 8145001

MCO P4790.1B Ch 1
LPP-3
21 Jan 92

MARINE CORPS ORDER P4790.1B Ch 1

From: Commandant of the Marine Corps
To: Distribution List

Subj: MARINE CORPS INTEGRATED MAINTENANCE MANAGEMENT SYSTEM
       (MIMMS) INTRODUCTION MANUAL

Encl: (1) New page inserts to MCO P4790.1B

1. <u>Purpose</u>. To transmit new page inserts to the basic Manual.

2. <u>Action</u>. Remove pages 4-5 and 4-6 from the basic Manual and
replace with corresponding pages.

3. <u>Summary of Chance</u>. To redefine the requirements.

4. <u>Chance Notation.</u> Significant changes in the revised pages
for this Change are denoted by an arrow (>) symbol.

5. <u>Filing Instructions</u>. This Change transmittal will be filed
immediately following the signature page of the basic Manual.

                                    R. J. WINGLASS
                                    Deputy Chief of Staff
                                    for Installations and Logistics

DISTRIBUTION: PCN 10206545001

          Copy to: 7000161 (100)
                    7000144 (1)
                    8145001 (1)

MCO P4790.1B CH 2
LPP-3
31 Jul 92

MARINE CORPS ORDER P4790.1B Ch 2

From: Commandant of the Marine Corps
To: Distribution List

Subj: MARINE CORPS INTEGRATED MAINTENANCE MANAGEMENT SYSTEM
        (MIMMS) INTRODUCTION MANUAL

Encl: (1) New page inserts to MCO P4790.1B

1. Purpose. To transmit new page inserts to the basic Manual.

2. Action

    a. Remove page iii and replace with the corresponding page
contained in the enclosure.

    b. Insert new Appendix A contained in the enclosure.

3. Summary of Change. To add a listing of maintenance related
programs to the basic Manual.

4. Change Notation. Significant changes in the revised pages
for this change are denoted by an arrow (>) symbol.

5. Filing Instructions. This Change transmittal will be filed
immediately following page 3 of the basic Manual.

                              R. J. WINGLASS
                              Deputy Chief of Staff
                              for Installations and Logistics

DISTRIBUTION: PCN 10206545002

        Copy to: 7000176 (100)
                  7000144 (1)
                  8145001 (1)

LOCATOR SHEET

Subj: MIMMS Introduction Manual

Location: _____
          (Indicate the location(s) of the copy(ies) of this
          Manual.)

RECORD OF CHANGES

Log completed change action as indicated.

Change Number	Date of Change	Date Received	Date Entered	Signature of Person Entering Change

MIMMS INTRODUCTION MANUAL

CONTENTS

MIMMS INTRODUCTION MANUAL

CHAPTER 1

INTRODUCTION

CHAPTER 1

INTRODUCTION

1000. <u>BACKGROUND</u>. The MIMMS is a set of manual procedures by which the effective use of personnel, money, facilities, and materiel as applied to the maintenance of ground equipment is controlled. It is supported by an Automated Information System (AIS) which functions as a stand alone Class I system that interfaces with existing Marine Corps systems and programs. MIMMS and MIMMS/AIS apply to all command levels and maintenance echelons. They provide management visibility to the user level while simultaneously collating maintenance engineering analysis (MEA) information for item management.

1001. <u>OBJECTIVES</u>. By providing visibility of maintenance resources, MIMMS enables commanders to prioritize assets to better accomplish the maintenance mission and thereby improve readiness. In support of this objective MIMMS:

1. Defines and establishes uniform management policies and procedures for ground equipment maintenance.

2. Improves staff planning, organization, direction, and coordination of maintenance activities.

3. Documents requirements, actions, and expenditure of resources.

4. Provides timely update of requirements status through system interface.

5. Provides timely management information for prioritizing operations and identification and correction of trends, excesses, deficiencies, and waste.

6. Provides readiness reporting information.

7. Extracts selected history for use in acquisition, budgetary, and item management decisionmaking.

1002. <u>GENERAL POLICY</u>

1. A commander is responsible for the operational readiness of table of equipinent (T/E) items and for maintaining them within the capabilities of his table of organization (T/O) mission statement. Intermediate and depot level maintenance activities are responsible to support that maintenance required beyond an organizational capability.

2. The same policies and procedures apply to all commands, all ground equipment commodity areas, and all echelons of maintenance as outlined herein:

    a. This Manual applies to all reparable items appearing on the appropriate T/E's, allowance lists and special allowances except as indicated below.

    b. This Manual does not apply to the following:

        (1) Aviation materiel furnished by the Navy which is subject to policy prescribed by the Chief of Naval Operations.

        (2) Medical and dental materiel which are subject to the maintenance policies of the Commander, Naval Medical Command.

        (3) Musical instruments maintained per the current edition of MCO 4225.2.

        (4) Industrial plant equipment which does not appear on T/E's or the current edition of NAVMC 1017 (table of authorized material (TAM)).

        (5) Garrison mobile equipment (GME) when specific procedures delineated in other manuals differ.

        (6) Development equipment.

        (7) Equipment used in the geo-prepositioning program.

    c. This Manual applies to Navy-furnished equipment maintained by the Marine Corps under Interservice Support Agreement (ISSA) or directive; e.g., helicopter mounted M6 .50 caliber and M60 machine guns, per the current edition of NAVMATINST 8300.1.

3. Ground maintenance shall be managed as outlined in this Manual, other manuals in the 4790 series, and as amplified by the directives of the CMC.

1003. SYSTEM ORGANIZATION. MIMMS/AIS has three subsystems: The Headquarters Maintenance Subsystem (HMSS), the Depot Maintenance Subsystem (DMSS) and the Field Maintenance Subsystem (FMSS).

1. HMSS. The HMSS provides a data base of standards information and selected maintenance information to support logistics managers

at Headquarters Marine Corps (HQMC), Marine Corps Research Development and Acquisition Command (MCRDAC), and the Marine Corps
Logistics Base (MCLB), Albany. Policy and procedures for the HMSS
are governed by the current edition of MCO 4790.7 and other HQMC
directives in the 4790 series.

2. DMSS. Policy for depot maintenance is contained in the current
edition of MCO P4790.3 (MIMMS Depot Policy Manual). The supporting information system (DMSS) is governed by the current
edition of MCO P4790.6 (MIMMS Depot Users Manual).

3. FMSS. Field maintenance policy and procedures are addressed
by the current edition of MCO P4790.2 and its supporting information system (FMSS) which is governed by the current edition of
UM 4790-5. Manual records and reports are the basic source for
much of the information provided to the FMSS. The current edition
of TM-4700-15/1 is the source document for all manual equipment
record procedures.

CHAPTER 2

MAINTENANCE DEFINITIONS AND PROGRAM EXPLANATIONS

CHAPTER 2

MAINTENANCE DEFINITIONS AND PROGRAM EXPLANATIONS

2000. <u>DEFINITIONS AND PROGRAM ORIENTATION</u>

1. <u>Maintenance</u>. Maintenance is that action taken on materiel to restore it to or retain it in serviceable condition.

2. <u>Program Orientation</u>. MIMMS is the means employed in the Marine Corps to accomplish and manage the maintenance of ground equipment through an integrated system encompassing all equipment commodity areas, based on standard policies and procedures. It is user-oriented and designed to work with other logistics systems.

2001. <u>BASIC ELEMENTS OF MAINTENANCE</u>. Maintenance is comprised of two elements: engineering and production.

1. <u>Maintenance Engineering</u>

    a. Definition. Maintenance engineering occurs throughout an equipment's life-cycle. It develops maintenance concepts, establishes criteria for equipment maintenance, and prepares the technical requirements used in the supply system to support items of equipment. Maintenance engineering bases its concepts and plans on past equipment history. This information can also be used to Identify requirements to modify equipment.

    b. Application. Maintenance engineering under MIMMS is incorporated into the overall Integrated Logistics Support (ILS) effort. ILS integrates maintenance with other support considerations; e.g., facilities, personnel, training, and technical data, to estimate the supply support requirements of equipment throughout its life-cycle.

2. <u>Maintenance Production</u>. Maintenance production is the physical accomplishment of maintenance functions which commences with the delivery of equipment to the user and continues until it is removed from the inventory. These functions are:

    a. Preventive maintenance (PM).

    b. Corrective maintenance (CM)

    c. Overhaul.

    d. Rebuild.

e. Modification.

f. Calibration.

g. Modernization.

h. Conversion.

2002. MAINTENANCE CATEGORIES. The Department of Defense (DoD) categories of maintenance production are organizational, intermediate, and depot maintenance.

1. Organizational Maintenance. That maintenance production, scheduled or unscheduled, which is the responsibility of and performed by the using unit on its assigned equipment.

2. Intermediate Maintenance. Intermediate maintenance is that performed by designated activities in direct support of using organizations. It includes calibration and repair/replacement of damaged or unserviceable parts and provides technical assistance, support through a secondary reparable float and/or contact team support to using organizations. Intermediate maintenance normally includes third and fourth echelon maintenance and in instances when supporting overflow organizational requIrements, may include second echelon as well.

3. Depot Maintenance. That maintenance requiring major overhaul or complete rebuild of parts, subassemblies, assemblies or end items, including the manufacture of parts and performance of required modifications, testing, and reclamation. Depot maintenance serves to support lower categories of maintenance by providing technical assistance and performing maintenance beyond their responsibility. Depot maintenance provides stocks of serviceable equipment by using more extensive repair facilities than are available in lower level maintenance activities. Fifth echelon maintenance is normally associated with this category and is scheduled to employ production and assembly line methods whenever practicable.

2003. MAINTENANCE ECHELONS. The Marine Corps further subdivides the maintenance categories into echelons of maintenance (EOM) to more accurately identify capabilities. In this way tasks most appropriate to the unit's available commodity personnel, tools, equipment, and parts can be identified.

1. <u>First Echelon</u>. That maintenance performed by the user or operator of the equipment. It includes the proper care, use, operation, cleaning, preservation, lubrication and such adjustment, minor repair, testing, and parts replacement as may be prescribed by pertinent technical publications, tools and parts allowances. There is no requirement to collect MIMMS data at first echelon.

2. <u>Second Echelon</u>. Second echelon maintenance is that work performed by specially trained personnel in the organization. Appropriate publications authorize the second echelon of maintenance, additional tools and necessary parts, supplies, test equipment, and skilled personnel to perform maintenance beyond the capabilities and facilities of first echelon. This includes performance of scheduled maintenance; diagnosis and isolation of readily traced equipment malfunctions; replacement of major assemblies/modular components which can be readily removed/installed and do not require critical adjustment; and replacement of easily accessible piece parts not authorized at first echelon.

3. <u>Third Echelon</u>. Third echelon maintenance is that authorized by appropriate publications to be performed by specially trained personnel either in an intermediate or organizational role. Third echelon includes diagnosis and isolation of equipment/modular malfunctions; adjustment and alignment of modules using test, measurement, and diagnostic equipment (TMDE); repair by replacement of modular components and piece parts which do not require extensive post-maintenance testing or adjustment; limited repair of modular components requiring cleaning, seal replacement, application of external parts, and repair kits; accomplishment of minor body work and evaluation of emissions of internal combustion engines.

4. <u>Fourth Echelon</u>. That maintenance normally associated to semi-fixed or permanent shops of intermediate maintenance activities and frequently associated to organizational shops of units with a commodity peculiar mission. Fourth echelon maintenance includes diagnosis, isolation, adjustment, calibration, alignment, and repair of malfunctions to the internal piece part level; replacement of defective modular components not authorized at lower echelons; repair of major modular components by grinding, adjusting, items such as valves, tappets, seats; replacing internal and external piece parts to include solid state integrated circuits and printed circuit boards/cards; and performance of heavy body, hull turret, and frame repair.

5. <u>Fifth Echelon</u>. That maintenance normally performed by depot maintenance activities and at intermediate maintenance activities when specially authorized by the CMC (LPP). It includes overhaul/ rebuild of end items/modular components; repairs which exceed the capability of lower echelon units where special environmental

facilities or specific tolerances are require4; nondestructive
testing; special inspection/modification requiring extensive dis-
assembly, or elaborate test equipment; manufacturing items not
provided or available, and provision of wholesale level direct
exchange support.

2004. <u>MAINTENANCE AUTHORITY</u>. T/O's indicate the maintenance
authority of each unit based on the capabilities, personnel and
equipment rated, and careful consideration of the unit's wartime
mission. Requests to exceed that authority must be similarly based
and may be granted only per the provisions of MCO P4790.2.

CHAPTER 3

MAINTENANCE MANAGEMENT PROGRAM PROCEDURES

CHAPTER 3
MAINTENANCE MANAGEMENT PROGRAM PROCEDURES

3000. GENERAL PROCEDURES

1. Equipment maintenance management shall follow the procedures
set forth in this Manual and other maintenance directives and
publications.

2. Repairs shall be performed at the lowest echelon/category of
maintenance and, in a tactical environment, as far forward as
possible. Choice of echelon/category shall depend on the type of
repair, time factors, parts required, and the tools, equipment, and
personnel available. Tactical conditions and temporary shortages
of support equipment/personnel may preclude a unit from performing
maintenance it is normally authorized to conduct. In such
instances, a higher maintenance category shall effect repair of
items evacuated to it, or provide support through use of secondary
reparable float, or by employing contact teams, as appropriate.

3001. SPECIFIC PROCEDURES

1. All organizations shall perform only those maintenance actions
which they are authorized to perform as indicated by their T/O.

2. Materiel requiring repairs beyond the scope or capability of
the unit shall be evacuated to the activity providing that capability.

3. Each echelon of maintenance incorporates the capabilities of
lower echelons and units authorized shall be required to accomplish
lower echelon tasks as well when practical or tactical situations
so dictate.

4. Units authorized lower echelons shall not perform maintenance
assigned to a higher echelon. Evidence of unauthorized maintenance
practices shall be reported to the proper commander for corrective
action.

5. Movement, protection, preservation, and general care of reparable materiel that is unserviceable shall be the same as that
afforded serviceable materiel to prevent further deterioration.

6. The time reparable materiel remains unserviceable and shall be
kept to a minimum.

7. Maintenance and maintenance management procedures shall not differ significantly for units whether in a deployed or garrison environment.

8. Information recorded on maintenance actions will be limited to those required by current publications. Maintenance management information shall be automated to the maximum extent possible to reduce manual recordkeeping.

9. Fleet Marine Force (FMF) units shall not perform fifth echelon maintenance except as specifically authorized by the CMC (LPP).

10. FMF commands and commands with combat related missions shall provide adequate maintenance time for subordinate units returning from combat, deployment, or extensive training operations to return to acceptable levels of combat readiness.

11. The supporting establishment, as defined in chapter 4, following, is exempt from those provisions of MCO P4790.2 which conflict with directives that specify policy and procedure for GME.

3002. <u>TRAINING PROGRAM</u>. Marine Corps formal schools will conduct MIMMS training for students who will operate, maintain, or supervise the operation and maintenance of ground equipment. This training will meet the following objectives:

1. Familiarization level training will be given to personnel who may become involved in MIMMS processes. The graduate should know the requirements and objectives of MIMMS; the Marine Corps organization of maintenance; and responsibilities of commanders, staff officers, and commodity specialists. They should be able to identify existing and proposed MIMMS manuals, know their general contents, and be familiar with MIMMS/AIS, including its input documents and output reports.

2. Operator/technician level training will teach students how to perform the maintenance and maintenance reporting appropriate to their grade and military occupational specialty (MOS). They should know the requirements and objectives of MIMMS, the Marine Corps organization of maintenance, and the responsibilities of the operator/technician in the maintenance program. They should be able to identify, locate, and use the necessary technical publications, be familiar with maintenance-related programs, know how the Marine Corps Standard Supply System (M3S) relates to maintenance, correctly identify and complete field level input documents, and use unit output reports.

3. Direct supervisory level training will enable supervisors to perform the management and supervisory duties appropriate to their grade and MOS. They should know the requirements for the operator/

technician regarding MIMMS, the responsibilities of personnel they will be supervising and their own responsibilities, andfunctions in relation to other command and staff sections. They should be able to determine the requirements for, acquire, maintain, and use technical publications. They should be familiar with maintenance related programs and know how to employ them in support of the maintenance effort. They must also be able to correctly complete field level input documents and effectively use unit output reports to identify trends, to prioritize their maintenance assets and allow for the most efficient production in support of their unit's mission.

4. Supervisory level training will enable graduates to perform duties commensurate with their grade and MOS. They should know the requirements described for the operator and direct supervisor as well as have a working knowledge of the AIS, the required input to support units whether in garrison or deployed, the means to obtain information from the data base, the AIS output, particularly at the major subordinate command level, and its managerial use for isolating trends and prioritizing production.

3003.   MAINTENANCE PRODUCTION PROCEDURES

1. General Information. Maintenance by a using unit will be accomplished within authorized echelons, governed by current capability, and consistent with the availability of maintenance resources. Intermediate maintenance will be effected through the established maintenance channels for the unit requiring support. When maintenance is not economically feasible within the organization or through normal intermediate maintenance channels, it may be necessary to acquire maintenance services via ISSA with other DoD activities possessing the capability and capacity for additional workload. Maximum use of government-owned, -operated or contracted facilities will be attempted before turning to commercial sources.

2. Maintenance Production by Field Units. Maintenance production in the field is restricted to first through fourth echelon maintenance. Actions performed will be limited to PM, CM, modification, and calibration.

    a. PM includes all servicing actions and those repair and test actions used in inspecting and detecting failures in initial stages before they develop into major defects. It includes all such actions whether conducted on a scheduled or non-scheduled basis.

    b. CM includes all repair and test actions performed on failed equipment to restore it to operating condition.

c. Modification includes all changes in design or assembly
which affect operation/configuration of equipment. Modifications
improve equipment functioning, maintenance, or safety of use.
Modifications of equipment will be made only at the direction of
the Commanding General (CG), MCLB Albany.

d. Calibration is the process by which the measuring ability
of a test or measuring instrument is checked against a certified
standard of accuracy and then adjusted accordingly.

3. <u>Maintenance Production by the Depot Maintenance Activity (DMA)</u>.
DMA's are authorized to perform all echelons of maintenance.
Functions in the DMA include overhaul, rebuild, conversion, and
modernization. The DMA's normally support the supply system on a
scheduled rebuild-and-return-to-stock basis. Their operations are
set up to employ economic batching or assembly line methods whenever
practicable.

4. <u>Maintenance Production Performed Under ISSA</u>. Marine Corps
activities may engage in ISSA's to provide maintenance production
for or obtain maintenance production from another military
department of DoD. Reimbursements are required in such cases.
Maintenance support agreements will be effected per existing DoD
directives.

5. <u>Maintenance Production Performed Under Cross-Service (Reim-
bursable) Agreement</u>. Marine Corps activities may engage in
cross-service agreements to provide maintenance production for or
obtain maintenance production from another military department of
the DoD. Reimbursements are normally required in such cases.
Maintenance support agreements will be effected per existing DoD
directives.

MIMMS INTRODUCTION MANUAL

CHAPTER 4

MAINTENANCE MANAGEMENT ORGANIZATION

CHAPTER 4

MAINTENANCE MANAGEMENT ORGANIZATION

4000. <u>GENERAL INFORMATION</u>.   This chapter outlines the Marine Corps maintenance management structure and the responsibilities of maintenance management officers (MMO's) within MIMMS. It also describes management responsibilities applicable to each level of maintenance within the FMF and the supporting establishment.

1. <u>Requirements</u>

    a. Commanders at all levels, including detached or separate commands, shall assign an MMO when their command is authorized second echelon or higher maintenance for more than one commodity area. The MMO shall coordinate and integrate the maintenance efforts of all command activities.

    b. The T/O's of battalion/air group size and larger FMF units reflect MMO billets or additional duty assignments by T/O line number. In comparable size units which require an MMO where the T/O does not identify the MMO billet, the commander shall assign an officer the duties of MMO. These responsibilities may be assigned as additional duty for an officer or as a primary duty for a staff noncommissioned officer when a full-time officer assignment is not required.

    c. In units authorized second echelon maintenance in only one commodity area, the individual designated as the commodity manager shall perform the maintenance management functions and need not be designated as the MMO.

2. <u>Responsibilities</u>

    a. <u>Commanders</u>. Commanders are responsible for the effective-ness of the maintenance program within their commands. Inherent in that responsibility is the requirement to:

        (1) Ensure that command attention is commensurate with maintenance's impact on the unit mission.

        (2) Provide standing operating procedures to direct unit efforts in support of the command maintenance program.

        (3) Ensure training programs are established which address MIMMS functional areas targeting operators, technicians, clerical, and supervisory personnel.

b. Organizational MMO. A unit MMO is responsible for the combined maintenance effort of the unit, whatever the echelon of command.   Responsibilities include oversight of system implementation, operation and evaluation of output to increase overall maintenance productivity, coordination of effective supply support with the unit supply officer, liaison with internal and external agencies on maintenance and maintenance related issues. The MMO will exercise staff coordination over commodity maintenance officers in matters not unique to a single commodity.

c. Support MMO. Like the unit MMO, the support MMO is responsible for the combined maintenance conducted by the unit but only as it functions in support of other units. This situation is normally restricted to service support organizations. The support MMO will supervise equipment maintenance production and resource management using data from MIMMS/AIS and other systems and programs. This MMO will coordinate support maintenance for the command with supporting and supported units.

d. Maintenance Information System Coordination Office (MISCO). The MISCO is the agency within the Marine Expeditionary Force (MEF) which coordinates the operation of Class I MIMMS/AIS between the using unit and the system sponsor.

4001. STRUCTURE ARRANGEMENT. Ground equipment maintenance management is accomplished on various levels existing throughout the echelons of command. These levels parallel the administrative command and functional equipment maintenance structures which exist in the Marine Corps.

4002. HEADQUARTERS MARINE CORPS. HQMC, Maintenance Policy Section (LPP-3), retains functional area responsibility regarding ground maintenance management policy. This office is responsible for coordinating with other HQMC staff elements, CG MCLB Albany, and CG MCRDAC, Quantico, whose functions relate to equipment/commodity peculiar requirements pertaining to maintenance planning and execution. As Maintenance Management Functional Sponsor this office also coordinates review of using unit system requirements and modifications with the system sponsor at Marine Corps Central Design and Programming Activity (MCCDPA), Albany.

4003. FLEET MARINE FORCES

1. Major Subordinate Commands. The Assistant Chief of Staff, G-4 at the force, division, wing, and force service support group (FSSG) has staff cognizance for ground maintenance management within the command and shall ensure an officer within the section is assigned the primary duty as the MMO.

2. <u>Regiments, Battalions, and Aircraft Groups</u>. In exercising responsibility for maintenance management, commanding officers shall ensure that an officer under the cognizance of the Logistics Section (S-4) is assigned the primary duty of MMO.

3. <u>Companies, Batteries, and Squadrons</u>. When the assignment of an MMO is not specifically required by the T/O, the commanding officer may assign an officer the additional duty of MMO. An MMO need not be assigned in the headquarters company of a battalion, regiment, or headquarters squadron of a group when the parent organization has assigned an MMO and maintenance functions are perf ormed under the cognizance of members of the executive/special staff.

4. <u>Service Support Units</u>

    a. The FSSG's have a threefold responsibility in coordinating organic maintenance, support maintenance, and Class I MIMMS operational requirements. FSSG commanders shall assign an officer in the G-4 to coordinate maintenance management functions appropriate to organizational equipment, an officer in the Combat Service Support Section to coordinate support maintenance requirements, and an officer in the Combat Service Support Section to coordinate Class I MIMMS operation.

    b. FSSG's, Brigade Service Support Groups, Marine Expeditionary Units, Service Support Groups, and Combat Service Support Detachments will be organized to include an officer to coordinate organizational requirements and a maintenance control officer in the Maintenance Operations Section to coordinate support maintenance requirements.

4004. <u>THE SUPPORTING ESTABLISHMENT</u>

1. <u>General Inf ormation</u>. The supporting establishment includes Marine Corps bases (MCB's), air stations, logistics support bases (excluding DMA's), districts, barracks, and other activities which are not part of the operating forces. Maintenance management as it applies to the supporting establishment is under the staff cognizance of the Assistant Chief of Staff G-4 or the S-4 at the appropriate level. The requirements for assignment of an MMO are no different from the operating forces. The following commands shall assign an MMO to coordinate maintenance of organizational equipment within the command:

    a. MCB's.

    b. Marine Corps schools authorized second echelon or higher in more than one commodity. If only one commodity is authorized second echelon, the commodity manager shall carry out the duties of the MMO.

    c.   Marine Corps Air Stations.

    d.   Marine Corps Recruit Depots.

    e.   MCLB's.

    f. Marine Barracks, Security Detachments, and Recruiting Stations when more than one commodity is authorized second echelon or higher. If only one commodity is authorized second echelon, the commodity manager shall carry out the duties of the MMO.

    g. Marine companies and squadrons may have an officer assigned the additional duty of MMO when required.

>2. <u>MISCO</u>. When supporting establishment commands opt to implement MIMMS/AIS, the MSC MMO shall coordinate implementation requirements with the supporting MEF MISCO, when collocated, or the supporting ASC, as appropriate.

4005.   <u>ORGANIZED MARINE CORPS RESFRVE AND INSPECTOR-INSTRUCTOR STAFFS</u>

1.   The 4th Marine Division/Marine Aircraft Wing/FSSG maintenance management programs parallel those of the active FMF organizations.

>2. MISCO responsibilities for the 4th Marine Division/Marine Aircraft Wing/FSSG will be accomplished by the 4th Marine Division MMO.

3.   Reserve unit responsibilities are the same as those assigned to like units of the regular Marine Corps. When a Reserve unit is subdivided geographically, officers shall be designated for each portion of the unit possessing second echelon capability or higher in more than one commodity.

> APPENDIX A

MARINE CORPS MAINTENANCE RELATED PROGRAMS AND SYSTEMS

This appendix contains maintenance related programs listing the program directive, the program definition, and the program's relationship to maintenance.

1. Configuaration Management Program, MCO 4130.8

    a. This program controls the function and physical characteristics of equipment throughout its life cycle. Configuration audits are used during development for an accounting of changes to equipment during its operational life.

    b. The Marine Corps Systems Command provides the maintenance engineering input for configuration management control decisions. Configuration audits provide maintenance engineering changes information. Maintenance engineering identifies the maintenance implication of equipment change proposals and documents them. Maintenance engineering evaluates the impact of changes on maintenance resources requirements and adjusts resources accordingly. Field units comply with the modifications and report them, when required.

2. Equipment Repair Criteria Program, MCO 4130.8

    a. This program determines which table of authorized materiel equipment will be repaired or replaced. It provides criteria which, when applied, avoid the unnecessary expenditure of maintenance funds when item replacement is more economical; and it establishes uniform criteria for retiring engineer equipment. The program places a one-time expenditure limit on equipment life expectancy. This figure is determined from the equipment's life expectancy and the in-use age at which it becomes eligible for retirement.

    b. Field units are guided by this program in performing equipment maintenance and equipment replacement.

3. Reliability Centered Maintenance Program, MCO 4700.3. This program is a basic element of maintenance management control and considers maintenance implications in equipment development. It ensures that effective maintenance is designed into equipment, sets parameters for maintenance requirements based on operational experience with equipment, and initiates technical changes or modifications to hardware.

4. Calibration Program, MCO P4733.1

    a. This program ensures that an accurate standards or measurement is maintained during the test, repair, and inspection of TMDE. Trained personnel in calibration facilities apply standards and calibration procedures to ensure that TMDE is accurately calibrated.

b. Timely calibration of test equipment and measuring instruments ensures that established standards of equipment performance remain exact during the equipment repair process.

5. Operational Readiness Float Program, MCO P4400.150

a. This program provides a pool of mission essential, maintenance significant end itmes used to provide replacement for unserviceable, reparable end items which cannot be repaired in time to meet an operational commitment.

b. Operational Readiness Float provides an interface between maintenance production and operational readiness. It allows a commander to maintain an operationally ready posture for mission essential equipment in the corrctive maintenance cycle.

6. Modification Control Program, MCO P4790.2

a. This program allows units to establish a modification control program. Required equipment modifications are published as MI's and listed in the Marine Corps SL-1-2 (MI's are announced in TI-5600). Information concerning GME modification will normally be provided by the manufacturer, as required.

b. The owning unit must ensure that all required equipment modifications have been completed and recorded in the equipment records per TM-4700-15/1.

7. Recoverable Items Program, MCO P4400.82

a. This program ensures recovery, evacuation, and disposal of reparable items that are in excess of unit requirements or that require repair at levels higher than the units authorized echelon of maintenance. Recoverability is also based on the condition of the materiel and equipment position of the Marine Corps on items not economically reparable.

b. Determining the condition of equipment nominated for recoverability is a maintenance production function. Unserviceable recoverable items will be considered for depot repair based on the findings of limited technical inspections conducted at field maintenance activities.

8. Quality Assurance Program, MCO P4855.4

a. This program supports unit readiness by improving service techniques and support procedures at the MCLB's. The program evaluates product quality. It establishes standards for detecting deviations from quality requirements and provides a feedback system to evaluate product quality. The effectiveness of quality assurance in product improvement results in better equipment readiness.

b. Maintenance contributes to this program by identifying and reporting equipment defects uncovered during rebuild, inspections, etc., at the repair activities. The Quality Assurance Program directly influences commitments to maintenance resources.

9. Rebuild Program, MCO P4400.82

a. This program provides a means for restoring unserviceable end items or secondary depot reparable items to serviceable condition for return to the operating inventory.

b. Management of the Rebuild Program is a function of maintenance production. Maintenance resources must be planned to support equipment restored through the Rebuild Program.

10. Secondary Depot Reparable Program, MCO P4400.82

a. This program provides for rapid restoration of deadlined critical items to a mission capable status by exchanging unserviceable secondary reparable items. Items in this category include subassemblies, modules, or major components for serviceable items retained in a preestablished location at an appropriate repair or reparable item issue point. The program identifies the items and establishes criteria for item use, repair, and evacuation and also promulgates reporting procedures for control of reparable issue point assets.

b. Maintenance facilities are the primary users of secondary reparable items. The secondary reparable items are used to restore equipment to a mission capable status. The maintenance activity repairs the unserviceable secondary reparable item and returns it to the reparable issue point allowance as a serviceable asset. Maintenance production personnel must also identify those secondary reparable items which are not economical to repair and report them to the MCLB's for disposition instructions.

11. Standardization Program, MCO 4120.5

a. This program improves equipment efficiency and readiness by adopting material and processes that have been evaluated and approved under qualitative standards and specifications. This reduces the number and variety of items in the inventory; conserves money, manpower, facilities, and resources; increases efficiency in design, development, materiel acquisition, and logistics support; and enhances the maintainability of military equipment and supplies.

b. The maintenance production effort benefits from this program by increased equipment reliability and reduced production time through parts interchangeability, quicker parts identification, and quicker supply support.

12. Technical Data Management Programs, MCO P4400.77

a. This program ensures a careful analysis of the necessary data requirements when procuring equipment. It controls procurement procedures and plans for effective equipment use by the Marine Corps. The Technical Data Management Program of the Marine Corps Unified Materiel Management System ensures that all catalog and support equipment information is procured, retrieved, and interfaced with other DoD programs and is continually updated. It also controls the publication of this information to the field.

b. The maintenance production element will identify new technical data requirements to support equipment maintenance. It will also assist in identifying discrepancies in existing data.

13. Quality Deficiency Reports Program, MCO 4855.10

a. This program is used to report equipment or materiel design and manufacturing deficiencies. Quality Deficiency Reports are submitted by equipment operators and maintenance personnel in the field. They report equipment performance defects or maintenance discrepancies with recommendations for improvement, whenever possible. The report is analyzed from an engineering standpoint; and, when appropriate a solution is issued to the field in the form of a technical or MI. When necessary, a change in equipment design is made for subsequent procurement.

b. The maintenance production element contributes to this program by:

(1) Identifying an equipment discrepancy and reporting it.

(2) Recommending possible solutions to the discrepancy.

(3) Performing applicable modifications resulting from Quality Deficiency Reports.

14. Value Engineering Program, MCO 4858.1

a. This program involves continuous and intensive appraisal of an item being procured and of all elements influencing its cost. The purpose is to eliminate or modify anything that contributes to the cost of the item but is not necessary to the required performance quality, maintainability, standardization, or interchangeability of the item.

b. The maintenance production element will identify unnecessary costs in the field and recommended changes. The maintenance engineering activity will evaluate change proposals from the field and from contractors and, when appropriate, will initiate action so that cost savings can be realized without jeopardizing equipment readiness. Changes, as a result of this program, are controlled through the Configuration Management Program.